The Frequency Of Everything

Tessa Ann

First published in Northern Ireland in 2016
by Excalibur Press

ISBN: 978-1-910728-33-8

Formatting & layout by
Excalibur Press

Excalibur Press
Belfast, Northern Ireland

team@excaliburpress.co.uk
07982628911 | @ExcaliburPress
www.excaliburpress.co.uk

Dedication to my friends, family, co-workers, audiences and clients who have supported me through my Sound Healing journey so far.

To Marianne Underwood, with whom I had my first ever Sound Healing experience in 2002.

To Tony Nec from The Sound Healing Academy for providing me with the training and continued support and many Sound Healing opportunities.

To Arts Ekta, Belfast for providing me with a platform to showcase Sound Healing in Belfast and continuing to support my work.

To Lorna Scott for her continued support.

Finally to Tina Calder from Excalibur Press for making this book possible and continuing to help me champion Sound Healing

CONTENTS

INTRODUCTION

This book, 'The Frequency of Everything' was inspired by my clients and audiences over the last four years.

Through their keenness to understand more about their experience with sound, why they hear or feel the sounds the way they do. Their wish to understand why a range of experiences can occur whilst listening to sounds in a relaxed state.

Therapeutic or healing sounds can feel irritating at times, as well as relaxing and this may be experienced for a variety of reasons.

With this awareness it allows you to alleviate any particular expectations you may have about a sound healing experience.

This book is what I term as an 'experiential book'. Bringing you the experience of working with therapeutic sound through listening to the accompanying recorded sound meditation 'The Frequency of Everything'. You will also receive a basic overview on Sound Healing and how it works in relation to other elements such as, 'vibration', 'energy' and 'setting intention'

It's important to notice how you feel during your listening experiences of the sound meditation. To notice what may be highlighted to you through the sounds you hear, through your awareness of sensations in your body or the energy around your body. As well as being aware of any thoughts that enter the mind each time you listen

Each experience can also be a experience of listening to 'the self', as well as the sounds. The sounds invite you to create a space for yourself, in order to tune in and listen to your own messages and intuition.

These messages are given to you in every moment, but are not always heard or acknowledged.

These messages may be brought into your consciousness through the experience of feeling sound and vibration in the body. Through the power of healing sounds.

Tessa Ann

WHAT IS SOUND HEALING?

Sound healing is a form of vibrational healing or vibrational medicine and is also known as Sound Therapy. It can be experienced in many different environments, as part of a group, as a one to one complementary therapy, or as self practice to reduce stress and improve overall well being whenever needed.

Sound is the fundamental nature of reality and every form has a unique vibrational frequency. Sound can be used as a therapeutic tool to balance all aspects of wellbeing, be it physical, emotional, mental or spiritual. Being out of balance means that aches, pains, illness and disease can set in. Sound therapy activates the body's natural healing mechanisms, helping to restore balance by using the vibration of sound.

Most people don't acknowledge how intuitive and sensitive the human body is. The human body is said to have its own vibration at which it resonates, with each part of the body having it's own specific vibration or frequency.

If a part of the body no longer resonates at its natural healthy frequency it becomes what may be referred to as 'imbalanced', 'out of tune' or 'off kilter'. This is said to cause aches, pains, disease, emotional imbalance, as well as other imbalances within the energetic and physical bodies.

The body naturally wants to feel balanced and in good health. It knows the frequency or vibration it requires resonate at in order to become well again and to maintain a healthy state. Upon meeting this frequency it requires for balanced health, (through sound healing for example) the body will draw in the frequency to help it return to a healthy state once again.

One of the most popular ways sound healing is delivered is through the playing of sound healing instruments and sounds, such as crystal singing bowls, Tibetan singing bowls, gongs, drums, percussion, stringed and wind instruments, natural sounds and voice. Not all of these sounds though have to be experienced at the same time, as they all play individual roles within the therapeutic sound session, creating a range of feelings and effects on those who experience them.

The range of vibration produced through the playing of these sound healing instruments is received by the body with the intention of restoring balance. Those parts of the body which are not in harmony can be brought back into harmony with the vibration of sound to help restore health and wellbeing.

While sound healing instruments play a key role in the therapy, 'intention setting' is another important aspect that is worked with when balancing and restoring the body.

Intention setting works with the vibration of words.

As everything carries its own unique vibration, so too does every word spoken. To set a beneficial intention, make it something that you 'desire' to have in your life at this moment, choose words that resonate with you and you can feel (as it's through this resonance, this feeling you believe these words to be true for you at this time) and set your intention in the present tense.

You can continue your own work with sound and vibration outside of any sound healing session, when you work with the power and vibration of intention.

A specific intention can be further amplified or boosted when it is combined with the frequency of healing sounds, through which transformation is often experienced.

Other effective ways in which healing sounds can be utilised and experienced are through listening to recorded sounds and also through the use of your own voice using a technique called vocal toning.

Clinical trials of sound healing have shown that sound therapy can help relieve insomnia, chronic pain, hearing difficulties, depression, anxiety, stress, high blood pressure, recovery from operation and much more. Sound healing promotes relaxation, balances the brain's hemispheres and improves overall well being, as well as easing specific areas of discomfort.

Sound healing has been beneficial to many people. Through this work I have documented many individual experiences as a way to support further research and development of sound as a therapeutic practice.

Vibration & Frequency

Vibration

Simple definition of 'vibration': "Vibration is a continuous, slight, shaking movement; a series of small, fast movements back and forth or from side to side." *(Merriam-Webster, 2015)*

Sound is vibration. A vibrating object creates sound waves which move through mediums such as air and water before the ear processes them as sound.

Vibration can often be felt in the physical and energetic bodies. In a sound healing session vibration may be felt in the body for many reasons.

When the body tunes into, or senses a vibration being played that it requires to bring it back into a healthy state of balance, the resonance of this vibration can sometimes be felt as the body draws it in.

As well as vibration being experienced through the hearing and feeling senses, it can also trigger colours, smells and images in the mind's eye.

Much of the sound and instruments played during a sound healing session create different types of experiences for each individual. The experience is often referred to as a sound journey on an energetic level whilst the physical body assumes a relaxed state.

Frequency

Sound is also a form of energy that travels as longitudinal (compression and rarefaction waves) through mediums such as air and water before our ears perceive this energy as audible sound.

In relation to sound, frequency is the number of sound waves produced in a second. It is measured from one crest of a wave to the next.

Hertz (Hz) is the unit of measurement for measuring frequency. So if a sound source produces sound waves at a speed of 5 cycles per second, the measurement for this would translate to 5 hz.

We also experience frequency through light waves and radio waves.

All matter is made up of energy, vibration and frequency.

Transforming Energy Through Vibration

The power of Vibration can be utilised in many ways. The process of Sound Healing uses sound vibration in a therapeutic way to promote relaxation, help bring about balance within the body and strengthen the energy that flows through the body.

It encourages a sense of wellbeing and can assist our bodies in returning to a natural healthy state.

Through the experience of listening to healing sounds, many individuals express what they call a 'letting go'. Whether this is the letting go of an emotion, a personal relationship, the ownership of a physical condition etc., the vibration of sound can support this process.

Through this 'letting go' of whatever you feel it is important for you to let go of in this present moment, you can then strengthen your own tower of energy. Your own 'Tower of Strength' within you.

The things you choose to hold on to are often referred to as 'entities', which are purely 'energy'.

When you choose to no longer hold on to the energy of an entity, such as a person, thing, condition, situation, emotion etc., it then creates space within you for your own unique life force energy to reside within you and run through you.

'Energy'

Energy is everywhere, and what science has shown us is that energy can neither be created nor destroyed.

It is just present in different forms.

www.one-mind-one-energy.com/energy.html

Through this process of letting go, not only do you strengthen yourself, but it also transforms the energy of that which you choose to release. Transforming it for the 'highest good of all.'

'Life Force Energy'

Natural life force energy is something that flows through all living things. It sustains and nourishes our bodies and can be used to support and increase the body's natural self-healing ability. This can speed up recovery from illness and injury. Life force energy can be used to boost our physical vitality and energy levels and to support and heal us on the emotional and psychological levels as well.

Life force energy is known as **chi** in China, **ki** in Japan and **prana** in India. It is also sometimes called **universal energy.**

www.life-force-energy.com

It is important to recognise that the things you choose to dwell on, can impact your personal energy. Dwelling on low-level situations can create a sense of low personal energy, or low personal power.

It's not that someone or something (entity) takes your power away from you, but because you choose to dwell on it, you in effect hand over your power to this entity, creating an experience of powerlessness within yourself, through your own intention of holding on to that, which no longer serves you.

Likewise, focusing on empowering experiences can create a sense of strength, motivation and steadfast personal power.

So energy, although it can neither be created nor destroyed, it can be transformed, into a form that will best serve you in this moment.

It is your choice, if you so desire, to make this transformation.

Remember that this choice can be supported by the power of vibration.

Having this awareness brings your power back to **YOU**. For **YOU** to be the one to decide, what the next step is for **YOU**?

Do **YOU** choose to continue to hold on or let go?

Transforming The Energy Of The Physical & Energetic Body With Vibration

As highlighted in previous chapters 'What is Sound Healing?' and 'Vibration & Frequency', I come back to the idea that everything is energy, vibration and frequency.

So, remember the concept that each body part resonates at its own frequency? So to do your thought processes, the energy that runs through your body, your actions, intentions, beliefs etc. I could go on here, but you hopefully get the idea.

Each of these elements link into the physical body, as well as what is referred as our 'energetic body'. The 'energetic body'. runs through the body as well as around and outside the body. The 'energetic body' may be felt, but may not be seen. Although some people may be gifted in a way, where they can visually experience the energy body.

Working with vibration can support and transform the vibratory rate of each of the abovementioned. Transforming the frequency at which they resonate, to bring it into line with what is healthy and balanced for the individual.

About Your Accompanying Recording:
The Frequency Of Everything

The main recording included with this book contains a variety of sounds that have been recorded by Tessa Ann from The Sound Healing Spa, including voice, Tibetan singing bowls, crystal singing bowls, percussion & the sound of water.

The sound of water itself produces a white noise effect. White noise is often used for masking other distracting sounds, as well as helping with sleep and relaxation.

In the context of this cd, the sound of water in the background helps to produce not only a relaxing effect, but a clearing effect on the mind and the energy of the of body, whilst listening to the other sounds in the sound meditation.

Combining all of the different frequencies of sound together at once produces 'white noise'.

White Noise:

A mixture of sounds or electrical signals that consists of all of the sounds or signals in a large range

www.dictionary.cambridge.org/dictionary/english/white-noise

As white noise contains the frequencies of all sounds, this particular sound meditation has been entitled: 'The Frequency of Everything'.

To download your 6 audio files to accompany this book log onto: *www.excaliburpress.co.uk/frequency-everything-downloads*

Preparation For The Healing Sounds Meditation

To download your 6 audio files to accompany this book log onto:
www.excaliburpress.co.uk/frequency-everything-downloads

As you prepare to listen to this recording, please take time to make yourself comfortable in either a seated or lying down position.

Consider what is right for you at this time, based on your environment, your mobility and what props you have available to you.

If you choose to adopt a seated position, you can use a chair, a meditation stool, or you can sit on a cushion in either a cross-legged position (or with your with legs in alignment with the body, knees bent, with feet planted on the floor) using a wall to support your back if required.

If you choose to lie down, you can use a comfy sofa, a bed or a yoga mat on the floor.

If you choose to lie on the floor, you may wish to consider your posture here especially if you experience discomfort in the lower back.

If this is the case for you, you may like to try the following for comfort:

- Lie with your back on the mat, bend the knees with

your feet planted on the floor (try moving the feet to a slightly wider position so that they sit on the edge of each side of the mat).

- Use a pillow and blanket if required.

- Make sure that you feel you are in a comfortable position to allow natural breathing.

Relaxing the body through the breath

To download your 6 audio files to accompany this book log onto: www.excaliburpress.co.uk/frequency-everything-downloads

Take some time here to focus on your breath.

Breathing in through your nose and out through your nose, if this is comfortable for you.

Direct your breath down towards your belly and notice how your breath starts to deepen.

Notice how your belly rises, as you breath in and notice how it falls, as you breath out.

Now with each breath in, start to scan your body for any areas of tension you may be holding on to at this time.

And with each breath out, allow those areas of tension to dissolve and relax.

Breathing in this way and releasing these areas of tension, allow the body to move into relaxation.

Once you feel ready, simply return to normal breathing. (Breathing that is normal for you, not forced).

Using the Vibration of Colour to Support You

To download your 6 audio files to accompany this book log onto: www.excaliburpress.co.uk/frequency-everything-downloads

Now I invite you to work with the vibration of colour before you listen to the sound meditation.

Allow a colour or range of colour come into your mind. Staying here with the first colour that comes to you.

It's important that you go with what first comes to mind, as this is a way for you to tune into exactly what you and your body need for support and nurturing at this time.

Visualise this colour surrounding your body.

As you are working with the Vibration of Colour here, you may feel the colour or range of colour that you have chosen start to resonate with certain areas of your body or your energy around the body.

If it is a challenge for you to visualise colour, then simply bring in the name of the colour, as the name will also carry the same vibration of the colour that you've chosen.

I also invite you in this moment to bring in the Vibration of Unconditional Love, again as a colour.

But go with the colour that represents the Vibration of Unconditional Love for you.

This High Vibration will help to nurture you and nourish you during this experience and you can choose to bring in colour on a daily basis to continue the process of self-nurturing.

Working with the Vibration of Words

To download your 6 audio files to accompany this book log onto: www.excaliburpress.co.uk/frequency-everything-downloads

Now that you have taken the time to work with the Vibration of colour, we will move on to working with the Vibration of Words, through setting an intention.

What is intention?

An intention is a statement for that which you desire to have in your life at this present moment. It is important to set this intention for the 'highest good of all', without any attachment to the outcome.

Again, if you find it a challenge to choose a specific intention at this time, you could consider the following examples:

- Is there an emotional experience that you would like to release?

- Would you like to reduce the symptoms of a physical condition, that you are experiencing?

- Are you experiencing a personal situation or

relationship that you would like to see transformed?

- Do you seek clarity around a decision that you wish to make?

These examples may help you choose an intention that is right for you to set in this moment.

When setting your intention, it is important to set it in the present tense, as this will help you to align with the vibration of this intention, in this present moment.

Choosing words such as 'I AM', or 'I HAVE', for example, help to set your intention in the present tense.

Finally, choose the words that resonate with you.

If you choose the words that resonate with you, then this means that you believe these words to be true for you at this time.

You can state this intention inwardly or out loud. Just go with what YOU feel is right YOU.

Now you have stated your intention.

Sit with the Vibration of these words for a few moments and feel the power and the resonance of the words you have chosen.

Then simply let your intention go, so that it may be further amplified by the power of the Healing Sounds played during this Sound Meditation.

Listen To The Sounds

You are now ready to listen to the main meditation.

At the end of the Sound Meditation take a few moments to bring your awareness back into your body and noticeably feel your energy settle into your body once more.

*NB

A 2nd, 5 minute track with some percussion sounds has also been provided, if you feel that you require that bit of extra sound and time just to settle your energy, before you go about your day. (This may be useful if you are listening to this recording in the morning time or at any stage during the day).

To download your 6 audio files to accompany this book log onto:
www.excaliburpress.co.uk/frequency-everything-downloads

Short Exercise When You're On The Go

A very powerful way of working with Vibration is to work with the Vibration of Words (as you did when you set your intention for the meditation).

A very simple way to do this is by observing your thoughts. Observing your self talk, your inner voice. Observing how you communicate with others through your choice of words.

Observing how you physically feel during or after your self talk or your exchange of words with another.

The power of words can affect our bodies in a way most of us aren't even aware of.

By becoming aware of our communication with self and others, we can then start to become aware of the words we choose to use. Words that will create a different experience for ourselves and those around us.

Try this as a short exercise at home, sitting on the bus, in your place of work... and just notice how different your interactions with others become.

Notice the impact this has on you personally, as well as those around you.

Enjoy!

How You Can Experience Sound Healing

One-To-One Sound Therapy Sessions

What Happens during a One to One Session?

One to one sessions are designed to focus on nurturing the individual, on the physical, emotional or spiritual level. Often all three. Sound and vibration can have a positive effect on a range of conditions and issues.

The session begins with an initial consultation, followed by a Sound Therapy Treatment, then space is created for reflection / feedback at the end of the session.

Instruments used in the Sound Therapy Treatment include Tibetan singing bowls, crystal singing bowls, gongs, percussion drums and tuning forks.

A safe, secure and relaxed environment is created, so that healing can begin to take place.

One to one sessions can also be delivered as part of a mobile service.

Group Sound Bath Relaxation Sessions

What happens during a Sound Bath Experience?

Through a deep, relaxing journey with sound, our sound baths provide the ultimate relaxation experience.

You'll be surrounded by beautiful sounds of Tibetan singing bowls, crystal singing bowls, gongs, drums and voice, while enjoying a wonderful experience of sound and oneness.

During this experience you are invited to sit or lie down or sit to experience and feel the benefits of the healing sounds.

A space is held for reflection and connection at the end of each session.

The Sound Bath Experience is delivered to small and large groups.

Both to private groups, as well as public events.

Workshops & Training

Workshops

Basic introduction to working with sound therapy instruments. The workshops are designed to give you the opportunity to play these instruments and gain a better understanding of their effect.

Experience the satisfaction of generating the sounds for your own increased sense of health and well-being.

Training

Tessa Ann is an Associate Teacher with The Sound Healing

Academy, through which she will be delivering a schedule of Sound Therapy Training Courses across Ireland

Information on future dates can be found at:
www.thesoundhealingspa.com/soundhealingacademyireland

Retreats

Day and Week-end Sound Healing Retreats can be experienced through The Sound Healing Spa at various locations throughout the year.

These retreats provide the perfect environment to totally immerse yourself in transformational sounds, as well as the opportunity for space, nature and other featured therapies and techniques based on the theme of the retreat at the time.

Information on up and coming events can be found at:
www.thesoundhealingspa.com/category/events

Events

The Sound Healing Spa provides a range of experiences through events, festivals and programmes.

Events include:

Sound Bath Experiences, Electronic Sound Bath, Ascension Events & Wellbeing / Festival Events.

Information on up and coming events can be found at:
www.thesoundhealingspa.com/category/events

What Is A Sound Bath?

A Sound Bath is usually a session delivered to a group and although it is mainly used for relaxation, many individuals can have profound experiences during these sessions.

When Tessa delivers her Sound Bath Sessions, she plays a range of instruments to produce different effects throughout the journey.

It will introduce you to the effects that different types of musical instruments can have on the body, when played with the intention of using them sound as a therapeutic tool. After a Sound Bath some individuals often describe their experience as one of feeling bathed in sound, or a feeling of sound washing over them.

Even in a group environment, each person will have their own individual experience of the sounds.

For some this is felt physically, for others it works on an emotional or mental level. The session may also be experienced in a more spiritual way.

There is no set or specified way that one should experience a Sound Bath session.

The instruments Tessa plays include, Tibetan and crystal singing bowls for deep relaxation, her voice to cover a wide range of frequency and vibration, percussion instruments such as shakers and rainsticks to waken up the body and help the body's energy to flow and the drum to ground the body's energy.

There is an in-exhaustive list of Sound Therapy instruments and Tools available to work with and a Sound Therapy practitioner will be drawn to use a certain instrument for a particular purpose or with a specific intention.

What is the difference between a one to one session and a Sound Bath?

A one to one Sound Healing session is different to that of the group Sound Bath experience, as a one to one session allows for much deeper work due to personal factors, which are brought into the session and the intention of working with that one specific person and their life experience in that moment.

It allows for exploration and transformation, that wouldn't generally be explored within a group environment.

About Tessa Ann

Tessa Ann has worked in the area of sound and music for over 20 years. She now combines this love of sound with her passion for wellbeing and complementary therapies to practice as a Sound Therapist in her business The Sound Healing Spa.

Organising various wellbeing events and workshops alongside her delivery of sound healing to individuals and groups, Tessa continues to increase her skills and knowledge, through her own continued personal and professional development. To help inspire creativity within her work she combines her sound healing practice with her holistic personal training and coaching services.

Tessa's focus is always on creation, be it creating a space for people to chill and relax, or by creating opportunities for others to be involved in her events.

Her sessions and events range from relaxation sessions, through to events where people can be more interactive, have fun and be inspired through movement as well as sound.

Sound is vibration and Tessa plays a range of sound healing instruments to produce vibration that can resonate with the body's own vibrations promoting relaxation, balance, and connection to the self. Through this process people can experience great benefits and healing on many levels.

Bringing these experiences to people every day has been a

rewarding experience for Tessa as she herself now has, and promotes, a more balanced lifestyle.

Having lived with a Pituitary Adenoma for 14 years, Tessa has now been given the all clear and attributes her wellness to the energetic work she has done for herself, as well as through the work she has delivered to others. It has shown her the benefits that one can gain for the self, when one works with the intention of the betterment of others.

As Tessa still loves to DJ, her latest creative project sees her combining her passion for sound therapy work with DJ'ing and electronic music production to create her 'Electronic Sound Bath'. Providing the experience of healing sounds in a more upbeat environment, allowing her to reach a wider audience.

Contact Me

To book a one-to-one or telephone consultation with Tessa Ann from The Sound Healing Spa call +44 (0)7792 925 128 or email info@thesoundhealingspa.com

Connect with The Sound Healing Spa on Facebook
www.facebook.com/soundhealingspa/events

Follow us on Twitter
www.twitter.com/SoundHealingSpa

Website
www.thesoundhealingspa.com/category/events